MAD SCIENTIST:
riddles·jokes·fun

by **JOSEPH ROSENBLOOM**
ILLUSTRATIONS by **SANFORD HOFFMAN**

 Sterling Publishing Co., Inc. New York
Distributed in the U.K. by Blandford Press

Also by Joseph Rosenbloom

Bananas Don't Grow on Trees
Biggest Riddle Book in the World
Daffy Dictionary
Doctor Knock-Knock's Official Knock-Knock Dictionary
Funny Insults & Snappy Put-downs
Gigantic Joke Book
How Do You Make an Elephant Laugh?
Looniest Limerick Book in the World
Monster Madness
Polar Bears Like It Hot
Ridiculous Nicholas Pet Riddles
Ridiculous Nicholas Riddle Book
Silly Verse (and Even Worse)

Library of Congress Cataloging in Publication Data

Rosenbloom, Joseph.
  Mad scientist.

  Includes index.
  Summary: A collection of riddles, jokes, and
tongue twisters featuring scientists, doctors,
robots, computers, space creatures, and other
scientific and science fiction phenomena.
    1. Riddles, Juvenile.   2. Wit and humor,
Juvenile.   [1. Science—Wit and humor.   2. Science
ficton—Wit and humor.   3. Riddles.   4. Jokes]
I. Hoffman, Sanford, ill.   II. Title.
PN6371.5.R6125   1982   818′.5402   82-50555

ISBN 0-8069-4662-8
ISBN 0-8069-4663-6 (lib. bdg.)
ISBN 0-8069-7804-X (pbk.)

Contents

To Leonard and Adrienne Backerman

1 Blasting Off

How did Mary's little lamb get to Mars?
By rocket sheep.

What travels around the earth all year
without using a drop of fuel?
The moon.

Why is the moon like a dollar?
Because it has four quarters.

What do astronauts do when they get
angry?
They blast off.

What would you get if the cow that jumped over the moon fought Taurus the Bull?

Steer Wars.

Why was the astronaut wrong when he landed on the moon and reported there was no life there?

There was—with him on it.

What did the Mad Scientist get when the rocket fell on his foot?

Mistletoe.

How do you put a baby astronaut to sleep?

You rock-et.

What do you call a person who is crazy about going into space?
An astro-nut.

What do you call an astronaut who is afraid of heights?
A failure.

Why did the astronaut lie on the bed before he blasted off?
He wanted to count down.

What do little astronauts get when they do their homework?
Gold stars.

Who was the first settler in the West?
The sun.

Which is lighter: the sun or the earth?
The sun, because it rises every morning.

What kind of bath does the Mad Scientist take without water?
A sun bath.

How does the Mad Scientist tune into the sun?
With a sundial.

What does the sun do when it gets tired?

It sets a while.

What does an astronaut do when he gets dirty?

He takes a meteor shower.

What is the secret of being a happy astronaut?

Never look down.

What is an astronaut's favorite meal?

Launch.

What is round and purple and orbits the sun?

The Planet of the Grapes.

What did the Mad Scientist get when he crossed a galaxy and a toad?

Star warts.

Which is the noisiest planet?

Saturn, because it has so many rings.

How do you get to the Planet of the Apes?

By banana boat.

What did the Mad Scientist get when he crossed a banana and a comedian?

Peels of laughter.

What did the Mad Scientist get when he crossed a banana and a bell?

A banana you can peel more than once.

How is a prisoner like an astronaut?
They are both interested in outer space.

How is Lassie like a comet?
Both are stars with tails.

What do you call a spaceman who is invisible?
An astro-naught.

Two astronauts were in a space craft circling thousands of miles above the earth. According to plan, one astronaut was to leave the ship and go on a 15-minute space walk. The other was to remain inside.

After completing his walk, the first astronaut tried to get back inside, but the door was locked. He knocked. There was no answer. He knocked louder. Still no answer. He pounded with all his might.

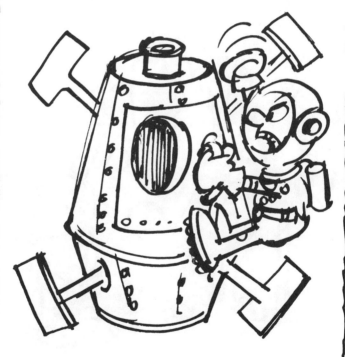

Finally, after what seemed like hours, a voice from inside the space craft spoke up: "Who's there?"

MAD SCIENTIST: Forget the moon—
everybody is going to the moon.
We'll go directly to the sun.

PILOT: We can't go to the sun. If we got
within 13 million miles of the sun, we'd
melt.

MAD SCIENTIST: Okay, so we go at night.

Why can't elephants become astronauts?
*Because their trunks won't fit under
the seat.*

Who really likes to be down and out?
A seasick astronaut.

Mad Scientist Dares you to Say These 3 Times Quickly

The charming chap chiefly sells cheap chipped rocketships.

Seth's sharp spacesuit shrank.

"Sure, the spaceship's ship-shape, sir!"

The spaceship's chief cheap sheep section.

The spaceship's back brake-block broke.

Why did the Mad Scientist pinch the waitress?

He wanted to see some flying saucers.

Why do astronauts wear bullet-proof vests?

To protect themselves against shooting stars.

ASTRONAUT: Wanna' fly?
COPILOT: Sure.
ASTRONAUT: Wait a second—I'll catch one for you.

2 Mad Doctors

REPORTER: Doctor, what is the best thing to do when your ear rings?

MAD DOCTOR: Answer it.

REPORTER: Doctor, what is the best way to prevent diseases caused by biting insects?

MAD DOCTOR: Don't bite any.

NURSE: Shall we give the patient a local anesthetic, doctor?

MAD DOCTOR: No, I'm in a hurry. Let's give him the express.

MAD DOCTOR: What is your problem?

PATIENT: I like bow ties.

MAD DOCTOR: Is that all? Thousands of people like bow ties. I prefer them myself.

PATIENT: You do? What a relief! How do you like them, boiled or fried?

MAD DOCTOR: You have a condition called "Updoc."

PATIENT: What's "Updoc?"

MAD DOCTOR: Nothing much. What's up with you?

What did the Mad Doctor say to the patient when he finished the operation?
   "That's enough out of you!"

MAD DOCTOR: The operation will cost you $400.

PATIENT: Can't you do it for $200?

MAD DOCTOR: Sure. But for $200, I use duller knives.

What bee is necessary to your health?
   Vitamin B.

When does the Mad Doctor charge his batteries?

When he can't pay cash.

MAD DOCTOR: Please breathe out three times.

PATIENT: Is that so you can check my lungs?

MAD DOCTOR: No, so I can clean my eyeglasses.

What would you get if your doctor became a vampire?

More blood tests than ever.

MAD DOCTOR: Nurse, did you take the patient's temperature?

NURSE: Why, no, doctor. Is it missing?

REPORTER: Doctor, what do you talk about with the zombie that you created?

MAD DOCTOR: Not much. I never learned to speak any dead languages.

REPORTER: Doctor, what's the difference between ammonia and pneumonia?

MAD DOCTOR: Ammonia comes in bottles; pneumonia comes in chests.

REPORTER: Doctor, what do you think of artificial respiration?

MAD DOCTOR: Personally, I prefer the real thing.

REPORTER: Doctor, why do you always wear a tuxedo in the operating room?

MAD DOCTOR: I like to dress formally for openings.

OPERATING ROOM

When they take out your appendix, they call it an appendectomy. When they take out your tonsils, they call it a tonsillectomy. What do they call it when they remove a growth from your head?
   A haircut.

Nurse to Mad Doctor: Doctor, you must learn not to cut so deep. This is the third table you've ruined this month.

Why did the Mad Doctor operate in the church?

He wanted to perform an organ transplant.

27

PATIENT: Doctor, I'm scared. This is my first operation.

MAD DOCTOR: I know how you feel. This is my first operation, too.

What does the Mad Doctor give a sick bird?

Tweetment.

LEM: What is a polygon?

CLEM: A missing parrot.

Where do they take care of sick parrots?

In a polyclinic.

PATIENT: I snore so loud, doctor, I can't fall asleep. What should I do?
MAD DOCTOR: Sleep in the next room.

MAD DOCTOR: I want to take out your appendix this evening.
PATIENT: That's okay with me, but please bring it home early.

What does a Mad Doctor do with a sick zeppelin?
He tries to helium.

What mental illness does Santa suffer from?
Claustrophobia.

According to a new scientific theory, exercise kills germs. The only problem is getting the germs to exercise.

What do you tell a germ when it fools around?
"Don't bacilli!"

What does the Mad Doctor do when a health nut knocks on the laboratory door?
Vitamin.

What boat takes dentists on short trips?
The Tooth Ferry.

When does a Mad Doctor buy a
thermometer?
Winter, because then it is lower.

What would you get if the Mad Doctor
swallowed a clock?
A tick doc.

MAD SCIENTIST: I saw a doctor today
about my memory.
IGOR: What did he do?
MAD SCIENTIST: He made me pay in
advance.

MAD SCIENTIST: Imagine you were strapped to an operating table with Dr. Frankenstein about to transplant your brain. What would you do?

IGOR: Quit imagining!

3 Mad about Martians

What is covered with ribbons and bows and comes from outer space?
A gift-wrapped Martian.

Two businessmen met on the street.

"Sam," said one, "have I got a bargain for you! I can get you a full-grown Martian for $50!"

"How big is this Martian?" Sam asked, trying to hide his interest.

"He's 10 feet tall and weighs 5 tons."

"Are you nuts!" Sam shook his head. "You know I live on the top floor of an apartment building with my wife and 4 children. What do I want with a 10-foot-tall Martian who weighs 5 tons?"

"You drive a hard bargain. How about two Martians for $75?"

Sam smiled. "*Now* you're talking!" he said.

What is better than presence of mind when a Martian aims a death-ray gun at you?

Absence of body.

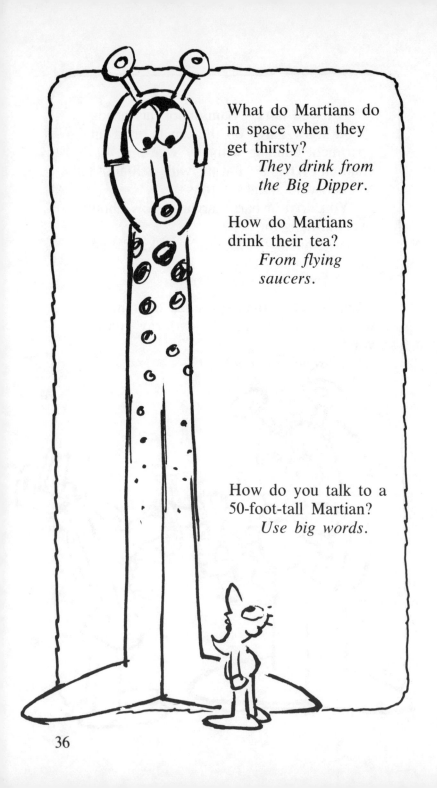

What do Martians do
in space when they
get thirsty?
*They drink from
the Big Dipper.*

How do Martians
drink their tea?
*From flying
saucers.*

How do you talk to a
50-foot-tall Martian?
Use big words.

36

MARTIAN: Are you tan from the sun?
ASTRONAUT: No, I'm Sam from the earth.

How do you arrange for a trip to Mars?
   You planet (plan it).

Two Martians landed in the Atlantic Ocean.
One said, "Hey, man, look at all that
water."
   The second Martian thought for a
moment and said, "Yeah, and that's only
the top."

MAD SCIENTIST: What is the difference
      between a Martian and a *pottfer?*
IGOR: What's a *pottfer?*
MAD SCIENTIST: It's to cook in, silly.

When are soldiers like people from outer space?

When they're Martian along.

CLEM: That star over there is Mars.
LEM: No, it isn't. It's Pa's.

A Martian spaceship crashed in the desert. The pilot and his copilot escaped without injury. However, after looking over their damaged ship, they were discouraged.

"We'll never get back home to Mars," sobbed the Martian copilot. "Our ship is useless. Our engines are smashed. What are we going to do?"

"Don't panic," said the pilot. "We'll figure something out. After all, four heads are better than one."

What would you get if you crossed a 50-foot Martian and a 300-pound chicken?
The biggest cluck in the solar system.

What did the Martian say when he landed in a field of weeds?
"Take me to your weeder."

MAD SCIENTIST: What do you say when a Martian walks up to you with a death-ray gun?

IGOR: I give up.

MAD SCIENTIST: That's right. Only you say it faster.

Where do Martians leave their spaceships? *At parking meteors.*

Two men from Mars, the first to land on earth, stepped out of their spaceship near a large town. Pointing to the TV aerials on almost every house, one happily said to the other, "Look—*girls!*"

MAD SCIENTIST: What is the difference between a Martian and a *snoo?*
IGOR: What's *snoo?*
MAD SCIENTIST: Nothing much. What's *snoo* with you?

What is soft, white, and comes from Mars? *Martian-mallows.*

Mad Scientist Dares you To Say These 3 Times Quickly

Martian fleas flee flies fast. If Martian fleas flee flies fast, how fast do Martian fleas flee flies?

A freely flowing Martian fruit float.

Martians frequently favor flat fat-free fruit-flavored floats.

Shabby space soldiers shovel soft snow slowly.

To feed a Martian sheep soup, seek short sheep.

What would you get if a rooster fought a Martian?

Creamed chicken.

Two Martians set their spaceship down in the wild swamp country of Florida. In the middle of the night, one Martian woke up yelling that an alligator had bitten off his foot.

"Which one?" asked the second Martian.

"How should I know?" the wounded Martian moaned. "They all look alike to me."

4 Tips from Transylvania

What happened when the Mad Scientist fell into the lens grinding machine?
He made a spectacle of himself.

What book tells you about all the different kinds of owls?
Who's Whoo.

IGOR: What are nitrates?
MAD SCIENTIST: What you pay for a telephone call after 5:00 p.m.

Why did the Mad Scientist cross a mole and Dick Tracy?

He wanted to bring law and order to the underground.

Why does the Mad Scientist like bargains?
Because he's 50% off, himself.

Why does the Mad Scientist count his money with his toes?

So it won't slip through his fingers.

What geometric figure is the most dangerous?

A firing line.

What nationality are people from the Arctic Circle?

North Polish.

How did the Mad Scientist get rid of flies
in his laboratory?
He hired a good outfielder.

Why did the Mad Scientist shoot his car?
He wanted to kill the motor.

What is the difference between little kids
at Christmas and werewolves?
*Werewolves have claws on their
fingers; little kids at Christmas have
claws (Claus) on their minds.*

What is "mean temperature"?
Twenty degrees below zero when you don't have long underwear.

What doesn't get wetter no matter how much it rains?
The ocean.

Why did the ocean roar at the ships?
Because they crossed it so many times.

Why was the ocean arrested?
Because it beat upon the shore.

Why is the ocean so grouchy?
Because it has crabs all over its bottom.

What would you get if you crossed the ocean and a thief?

A crime wave.

What do two oceans say when they meet after many years?

"Long time no sea."

What's the most romantic part of the ocean?

The spot where buoy meets gull.

What dog likes to hang around scientists?
A laboratory retriever.

How does a Mad Scientist make a lighthouse?
He uses balsa wood.

What did the Mad Scientist get when he tried to reach the beehive?
A buzzy signal.

IGOR: Why are Australian bees polite?
MAD SCIENTIST: Because they know how to beehive (behave).

MAD SCIENTIST: Igor, where are you?

IGOR: Here in the closet.

MAD SCIENTIST: What are you doing there?

IGOR: Well, didn't you tell me to read *Dr. Jekyll and Hyde?*

Who is more amazing than the Mad Scientist who drank 8 sodas and burped 7-Up?

The one who drank Canada dry.

What is a worm's favorite opera?
*Rigoletto
(wriggle-etto).*

Why did the Mad Scientist want to be a comedian?

He heard comedians make dough out of corn.

Did you hear about the Mad Scientist's latest invention? It's a spinning top that is also a whistle. Now he can really blow his top.

What did the Mad Scientist get when he crossed a sheep and some chocolate candy?

A Hershey baa.

Did you hear about the Mad Scientist who was so absentminded he poured ketchup on his shoelaces and tied knots in his spaghetti?

What mysterious thing did the Mad Scientist see in the skillet?
An unidentified frying object.

What did the Mad Scientist get when he crossed a ballpoint pen and a hippopotamus?
The Ink-credible Hulk.

Mad Scientist Dares you to Say These 3 Times Quickly

The bad black bug's blood.

Good blood, bad blood.

Do scientists see thieves seize skis? If scientists see thieves seize skis, where are the skis the scientists see the thieves seize?

What did the Mad Scientist get when he crossed a sheep and a banana?
    A baa-nana.

Where do rivers sleep?
    In river beds.

When does a river flood?
    When it gets too big for its bridges.

What's in the Great Wall of China that the Chinese didn't put in it?
    Cracks.

5 Rocky Horror

What is a geologist's favorite dessert?
   Marble cake.

What sweet do geologists like?
   Rock candy.

What do you call a geologist who doesn't hear anything?
   Stone deaf.

What happens to a small stone when it works up its courage?
   It becomes a little boulder (bolder).

What did the Mad Scientist get when he crossed an airplane, an automobile and a dog?

A flying car-pet.

FIRST GEOLOGIST: I bet you ten dollars that my name is harder than yours.
SECOND GEOLOGIST: Okay. What's your name?
FIRST GEOLOGIST: Sam Stone. Your name can't be harder than that. I win.
SECOND GEOLOGIST: No, you don't. My name is George B. Harder.

Whose fault will it be if California falls into the ocean?

San Andreas' fault.

Where do geologists go to relax?
Rock concerts.

What is a geologist's favorite lullaby?
"Rock-a-bye, Baby."

How does the Mad Scientist make notes out of stone?
He rearranges the letters.

What did the Mad Scientist get when he crossed a bag of cement, a stone and a radio?
Hard rock music.

What does a geologist have for breakfast?
Rock-n-roll.

When are geologists unpopular?
When they are fault-finders.

When are geologists unhappy?
When people take them for granite.

What kind of car does a rich rock star drive?

A Rock-n-Rolls Royce.

What do archeologists talk about when they get together?

The good old days.

What did the Mad Scientist get when he crossed a watch and 4 cups of milk?

A quartz watch.

What did the Mad Scientist get when he crossed a breakfast drink and a monkey?

An orangu-tang.

What did the Mad Scientist get when he crossed a stone and a shark?

Rockjaws.

What did the Mad Scientist get when he crossed a rabbit and a stand-up comic?

A funny bunny that walks on its hind legs.

What did the Mad Scientist get when he crossed a Martian, a skunk and an owl?

An animal that stank to high heaven and didn't give a hoot.

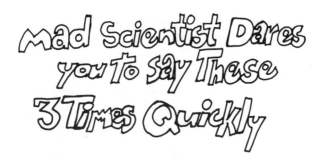

Thirty thin twin tinsmiths.

Twelve trim twin-track tape recorders.

Did the thin scientist throw three thick twigs?

Flee fog to fight flu fast.

Scientists flee free on three free through trains.

When is the moon heaviest?
When it is full.

How do you use a thermometer to find the height of a building?
Lower the thermometer on a string from the top of the building to the ground. Then measure the length of the string.

How many pieces of string does it take to reach the moon?
One, if it is long enough.

What did Whistler's Mother do when she met the Mad Scientist?
She went off her rocker.

What did the Mad Scientist get when he crossed a cat and a parrot?
A purr-a-keet.

What kind of music do you hear when you throw a stone into the lake?
Plunk rock.

6 Don't Feed the Robots

Why did the Mad Scientist put a rabbit in his automobile?
So he could use it for short hops.

When is a robot like a surgeon?
When it operates on batteries.

How does a Mad Scientist count cows?
On a cowculator.

FIRST ROBOT: Do you have any brothers?
SECOND ROBOT: No, only transistors.

What do you get when a robot's wires are reversed?
  A lot of backtalk.

What did the robot say when it ran out of electricity?
  "AC come, AC go."

How do robots cross a lake?
  In a row-bot.

What did the Mad Scientist get when he crossed a cow and a chicken?
  Roost beef.

What did the Mad Scientist get when he crossed a chicken and a cement truck?
  A hen that lays sidewalks.

What does a mechanical frog say?
  "Robot, robot!"

How does the Mad Scientist fix a robot gorilla?

With a monkey wrench.

What snacks should you serve robots at parties?

Assorted nuts.

What did the Mad Scientist get when he crossed a watch and a lollipop?

He got a watch that took a licking but kept on ticking.

What did the Mad Scientist write on the robot's tombstone?
"*RUST IN PEACE.*"

What did the little electric robot say to its mother?
"*I love you watts and watts.*"

Mad Scientist Dares you To Say These 3 Times Quickly

Will real wheels really wheel robots? If real wheels will really wheel robots, where are the robots that the real wheels really wheel?

Red leather robots, yellow leather robots.

Why did the Mad Scientist take his robot
to the psychiatrist?
Because it had a screw loose.

What kind of doctor operates on
Styrofoam robots?
A plastic surgeon.

75

BEST SELLER LIST

1. *Roller Coasters for Everyone* by Lupe de Lupe

2. *Astrology: What the Stars Mean* by Horace Cope

3. *Measuring School Work* by Tess D. Studenz

4. *Stunt Driving for Fun* by E. Rex Carr

5. *How to Get 100 Things Free* by Fern Otten

6. *Calming Werewolves* by Justin Casey Howells

7. *The Space Invaders* by Athena Martian

8. *Is There a Loch Ness Monster?* by Y. Knott

9. *The Big Bang Theory* by Adam Balm

10. *Reptiles Around the World* by Sally Mander

7 Zany Experiments

FIRST MOUSE: I finally got that Mad Scientist trained.

SECOND MOUSE: How so?

FIRST MOUSE: Every time I go through that maze and ring the bell, he gives me something to eat.

What did the Mad Scientist get when he crossed an electric eel and a sponge?
Shock absorbers.

What did the Mad Scientist get when he crossed a cow and an elk?
A wonderful place to hang milk pails.

What did the Mad Scientist get when he crossed a clock and a rooster?
An alarm cluck.

What did the Mad Scientist get when he crossed a porcupine and an alarm clock?
A stickler for punctuality.

How did the Mad Scientist make antifreeze?
He put ice cubes in her bed.

What did the Mad Scientist get when he crossed a parrot and an army man?

A parrot-trooper.

What was the football coach looking for in space?

An all-star team.

What did the Mad Scientist get when he crossed a small communist with a crook on horseback?

Little Red Riding Hood.

What is the most educated thing in the Mad Scientist's laboratory?

A thermometer, because it has so many degrees.

Why did the Mad Scientist throw the thermometer out of the laboratory on a hot day?

He wanted to see the temperature drop.

What did the Mad Scientist get when he crossed a banana and a banana?
A pair of slippers.

What did the Mad Scientist get when he crossed a comedian and a spiritualist?
A happy medium.

What did the Mad Scientist get when he crossed a reindeer and a firefly?
Rudolph the Red-Nosed Firefly.

What did the Mad Scientist get when he crossed a parrot and a canary?
A bird who knows both the words and the music.

What did the Mad Scientist get when he crossed a chicken and a television set?
A TV show that lays eggs.

What kind of jokes do scientists make?
Wisecracks.

What did the Mad Scientist get when he crossed a parrot and a bumblebee?
An animal that talks all the time about how busy it is.

Why didn't the Mad Scientist cross the Frankenstein monster with anything?
Because the Frankenstein monster doesn't like to be crossed.

Why didn't the Mad Scientist allow the sick eagle in his laboratory?
  Because it was illegal (ill eagle).

What animal won't the Mad Scientist allow in his laboratory?
  A cheetah.

How do you cut the ocean in two?
  With a sea-saw.

Why did the Mad Scientist put an elastic band around his forehead?
So he could stretch his imagination.

What did the Mad Scientist get when he crossed a sheep and a kangaroo?
Woollen jumpers.

What goes through water but doesn't get wet?
A ray of light.

IGOR: How long can a person live without a brain?

MAD SCIENTIST: How old are you?

What did the Mad Scientist get when he crossed a clown and a chicken?

A comedi-hen.

What did the Mad Scientist get when he crossed a sweet potato and a jazz musician?

Yam sessions.

BEST SELLER LIST

1. *How to Live in the Swamp* by Tad Pohl

2. *Foot Problems* by Aiken Bunyan

3. *Primitive Warfare* by Beau N. Arros

4. *Polar Exploration* by R.U. Cole and I.M. Freeson

5. *How to Use Space Weapons* by Ray Gunn

6. *Getting Started in Monster-Making* by Dr. Frank N. Stein

7. *You Can Be Healthy* by Colin D. Head

8. *How to Find Zombies* by Luke Sharp

9. *Mixing Chemicals* by Yul B. Sari

10. *A Tourist's Guide to Transylvania* by Bea Ware

8 Boys, Girls & Microchips

What did one volcano say to the other volcano?

"*I lava you.*"

What did one magnet say to the other magnet?

"*You attract me.*"

Two Martians landed on a corner with a traffic light.

"I saw her first," one Martian said.

"So what?" said the other, "I'm the one she winked at."

FIRST MAD DOCTOR: How was the science fiction movie you saw?

SECOND MAD DOCTOR: You know, the same old story: boy meets girl—boy loses girl—boy builds new girl . . . .

What does a computer call its mother and father?

Mama and data.

What does a proud computer call his little son?

A microchip off the old block.

What happened when the Mad Scientist threw an elastic band into the computer?

It gave snappy answers.

What happens if you cross a midget and a computer?

You get a short circuit.

What would you get if you crossed a computer and a kangaroo?

I don't know what you would call it, but it would always jump to conclusions.

What is a digital computer?

Someone who counts on his fingers.

Where do computers keep their money?

In memory banks.

What do you get if you cross an elephant and a computer?

A ten-thousand-pound know-it-all.

Why did the farmer put a computer in the hen house?

To make the chickens multiply faster.

What kind of royal cat do you find in a computer?

A Sir Kit (circuit).

MOTHER: I think Junior is going to be an astronaut.

FATHER: What makes you think so?

MOTHER: I spoke to his teacher today, and she said all he's good for is taking up space.

LITTLE BOY: I know someone who thinks
   he's an owl.
MAD SCIENTIST: Who?
LITTLE BOY: Now I know two people.

What home computers grow on trees?
   Apples.

"I've invented a computer that is almost
human," boasted the Mad Scientist to
Igor.
   "You mean it can think?" Igor asked.
   "No, but when it makes a mistake, it
puts the blame on some other computer."

Why didn't the Mad Scientist need a pocket calculator?
Because he already knew how many pockets he had.

When did Doctor Frankenstein stop being lonely?
When he learned how to make new friends.

Mad Scientist Dares you To Say These 3 Times Quickly

Brainy boys bake bad black bran bread.

Six sick scientists seek six crisp snacks.

Should a scientist shave a short single shingle thin, or shave a short thin single cedar shingle thinner?

When will a mathematician die?
When his number is up.

What kind of beat do mathematicians like to dance to?
Logarithms.

What did the Mad Scientist get when he crossed a computer and a vampire?
Love at first byte.

What did the Mad Doctor use to fix a broken heart?
Ticker tape.

9 Lightning Strikes Out

If lightning strikes an orchestra, who is most likely to get hit?
The conductor.

What is the difference between electricity and lightning?
You have to pay for electricity.

What does an electrician say when he goes to the doctor?
"Watts up, doc?"

What is yellow and goes "hmmm?"
An electric lemon.

What is long and yellow and always points north?
A magnetic banana.

How do you electrify a vampire?
With a bat-tery.

What did the Mad Scientist get when he
made an exact duplicate of Texas?
   A clone star state.

What song does an electric cowboy sing?
   "Ohm on the Range."

What did the Mad Scientist get when he crossed a porcupine and a young goat?
A stuck-up kid.

What did the Mad Scientist get when he crossed the Invisible Man and a cow?
Vanishing cream.

What did the Mad Scientist get when he crossed winter underwear and the Lone Ranger's horse?
Long John Silver.

What did the Mad Scientist get when he cloned and froze the Los Angeles Lakers' Abdul-Jabbar?
An iced Kareem clone.

What did the Mad Scientist get when he crossed a sailor and a dry cell?
Assault and battery.

When does a battery go shopping?
When it runs out of juice.

Why did the Mad Scientist bury the battery?
Because it was dead.

What does it mean when a barometer falls?
That whoever nailed it up didn't do such a good job.

Why did the Mad Scientist touch a live wire?

He got a charge out of it.

Why did the Mad Scientist study electricity?

He wanted to keep up with current events.

What did the Mad Scientist get when he crossed a frog and a soft drink?

Croak-a-cola.

What did the Mad Scientist get when he crossed an egg and a soft drink?

Yolk-a-cola.

How did the Mad Scientist try to fix a short circuit?

He lengthened it.

What did one raindrop say to the other raindrop?

"My plop is bigger than your plop."

10 Up and Atom

How do you count atoms?
You atom up.

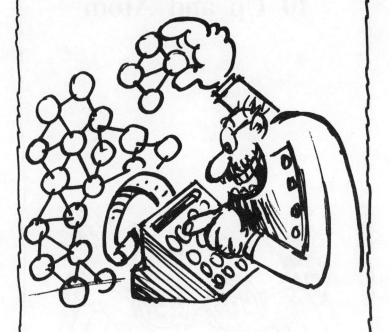

What is an atomic scientist's favorite snack?
Fission chips.

What do nuclear scientists argue about?
Whether splitting the atom was a wisecrack.

How do engines hear?
With engineers (engine ears).

MAD SCIENTIST: I see your new telescope only magnifies three times.

IGOR: Oh, no! I've used it twice already!

What is the quickest way to make oil boil?

Add the letter B.

Why was the Mad Scientist afraid of the letter N?

Because it is in the middle of TNT.

Where does the Mad Scientist raise magnets?

In magnetic fields.

What does the Mad Scientist add to a bucket of water to make it weigh less?
Holes.

What kind of water won't freeze in the Mad Scientist's laboratory?
Hot water.

What do you call it when Mother Nature
crosses an earthquake and a forest fire?
Shake and Bake.

What do you call a long series of
hurricane names?
A gust (guest) list.

Who does the ocean date?
It goes out with the tide.

How do you know when a big wave
wants to meet you?
The tidal (tide'll) wave.

Why did the Mad Scientist keep talking about the atom bomb?
He didn't want to drop the subject.

What is a hydrogen bomb?
Something that makes molehills out of mountains.

Why can't you play hide-and-seek with a mountain?
Because the mountain peeks.

How do mountains hear?
With mountaineers (mountain ears).

What is the longest distance you can see?
Down a road with telephone poles, because then you can see from pole to pole.

Why did the Mad Scientist go to the planetarium?
To see an all-star show.

How is an airplane like an atom bomb?
One drop and you're dead.

LEM: If we breathe oxygen in the
      daytime, what do we breathe at night?
CLEM: Nitrogen.

Why was the Mad Scientist puzzled every
24 hours?
  *He couldn't understand why night
  falls but day breaks.*

How do nuclear scientists relax?
  They go fission.

What figures do the most walking?
  Roman (roaming) numerals.

Why are mosquitoes great mathematicians?
Because they add to misery, subtract from pleasure, divide attention, and multiply rapidly.

Why are bacteria bad mathematicians?
Because they multiply by dividing.

Who was the first nuclear scientist in history?
Eve. She knew all about atom (Adam).

MAD SCIENTIST: A vacuum is the dirtiest thing in nature.

IGOR: How do you know?

MAD SCIENTIST: Why else would they make so many cleaners for it?

What is the difference between the North Pole and the South Pole?
All the difference in the world.

11 Mad Lab
Grab Bag

What kind of typewriter does Count Dracula use in his laboratory?
One that types blood.

What does the Mad Scientist measure that has no length, width or thickness?
The temperature.

The Mad Scientist invented a liquid that would dissolve anything it touched. He couldn't sell the invention, however. Why?
There was nothing in which he could put the liquid.

Which weighs more: a pound of lead or a pound of feathers?

They weigh the same—one pound.

What is H, I, J, K, L, M, N, O?

The formula for water (H₂O).

How many drops of poison can a Mad Scientist put into an empty test tube?

One, because after that it isn't empty any more.

IGOR: What is the most important rule in chemistry?

MAD SCIENTIST: Never lick the spoon.

Why doesn't the Mad Scientist trust the law of gravity?
Because it always lets him down.

What did the Mad Scientist find in the center of gravity?
The letter V.

Which is faster—hot or cold?
Hot—you can always catch cold.

What did the Mad Scientist get when he crossed an old car and a gorilla?
A grease monkey.

How does the Mad Scientist get a cow into a test tube?
He uses shortening.

What happened when the Mad Scientist put a young goat into the blender?
He got a crazy mixed-up kid.

What color is the wind?
Blew.

What kind of fish is in charge of an operating room?
The head sturgeon.

The Mad Scientist invented the most powerful glue in the world. He couldn't use it, however. Why?
He couldn't get the lid off the container.

How is a telephone like arithmetic?
> *One mistake and you get the wrong
> number.*

The Mad Scientist came to his laboratory
without a key and found all the windows
and doors locked. How did he get in?
> *He ran round and round the
> building—until he was all in.*

Why did the Mad Scientist throw the
chickens out of his laboratory?
> *Because they used foul (fowl)
> language.*

How many feet are there in a yard?
*(Most people will say three.) That
depends on how many people are
standing in the yard.*

IGOR: What would you say if I told you
that I had a bright idea?
MAD SCIENTIST: Nothing. I can't talk and
laugh at the same time.

What did the digital clock say to its mother?

"Look, Ma! No hands!"

What did the Mad Scientist get when he crossed a mummy and a stopwatch?

An old-timer.

IGOR: Do you have trouble making up your mind?

MAD SCIENTIST: Yes and no.

Why does the Mad Scientist wear sunglasses?

With all the Mad Scientist jokes in this book, he doesn't want to be recognized!

Index

127